Your Problem Isn't My Problem

By

Larry Richman

CENTURY PUBLISHING

SALT LAKE CITY, UTAH

Your Problem Isn't My Problem

ISBN 978-0-941846-38-7

Copyright © 2025 by Century Publishing, LLC

centurypubl.com

info@centurypubl.com

Printed in the United States of America.

Contents

Chapter 1: The Helper's Trap. *Why we feel responsible for other people's problems.* 4

Chapter 2: Boundaries Are Not Walls. *How to say "no" without shutting people out.* 8

Chapter 3: Enabling vs. Empowering. *How to help without harming.* 12

Chapter 4: Emotional Ownership. *Why we are not responsible for other people's feelings.* 15

Chapter 5: The Guilt Reflex. *Why we sometimes feel guilty.* 18

Chapter 6: When Helping Becomes Control. *Why sometimes the best way to help is to get out of the way.* 21

Chapter 7: The Myth of Martyrdom. *Why you don't have to earn your worth through burnout.* 25

Chapter 8: Letting People Learn the Hard Way. *How to let people face the consequences of their actions.* 29

Conclusion: Freedom in Responsibility 33

Preface

Most of us want to be helpful. We care. We show up. We try to support the people around us. But somewhere along the way, helping turns into fixing, supporting turns into rescuing, and caring turns into carrying burdens that were never ours to bear.

This book is about learning to tell the difference. It's about setting boundaries without feeling guilty. It's about letting people face their own problems—even when it's uncomfortable.

You don't have to save everyone. You don't have to carry what isn't yours. You don't have to feel responsible for what other people think, feel, or do.

This is a book about clarity, freedom, and peace—the kind that comes when you finally say: "Your problem isn't my problem."

CHAPTER 1

The Helper's Trap

Why we feel responsible for other people's problems.

We're raised to believe that helping is good. And it is. But too often, "helping" becomes overhelping. You offer advice they didn't ask for. You fix problems they didn't invite you to solve. You take on emotions that were never yours to manage.

Helping turns into rescuing. And rescuing turns into burnout. Then you feel drained, frustrated, or resentful.

This is the helper's trap: confusing *being responsible* for someone with *being responsible to* them.

- You are responsible *to* people—to be kind, honest, and respectful.
- You are not responsible *for* their reactions, choices, or emotions.

Real-Life Story (Workplace)

Melissa, a project manager, constantly picked up extra work when her teammates fell behind. At first, it made her look dependable. But over time, she grew bitter. Her team got used to her saving the day. She was enabling their lack of accountability—and exhausting herself.

The trap? Melissa confused being responsible *for* people with being responsible *to* them.

Real-Life Story (Parenting)

A mom keeps doing her adult son's laundry. He says he's overwhelmed. She thinks she's helping. But she's actually keeping him from learning how to manage his own life.

Real-Life Story (Friendships)

Ava's best friend frequently called late at night to vent about her problems. Ava always answered, losing sleep and feeling drained the next day. Eventually, Ava said, "I care about you, but I need to sleep to function. Can we talk in the morning?" Her friend adjusted—and their friendship survived just fine.

The common thread in all these stories? Each person thought helping meant carrying someone else's burden. But that's not help. That's hijacking someone else's growth process.

- You're responsible *to* others to be respectful, honest, and supportive.
- You're not responsible *for* their emotions, outcomes, or failures.

Tool: "Who Owns the Outcome?"

The next time you feel the urge to step in, ask: "Whose job is this really?"

If it's not yours, take a step back. Offer support—but don't carry what isn't yours.

Tool: The Internal Check-In

Ask yourself:

- Am I helping to feel needed?
- Am I afraid they'll be upset if I don't help?
- Am I doing this to avoid feeling uncomfortable?

If your help is about your need for control or comfort, it's probably not healthy help.

Key Takeaway

Helping becomes enabling when it removes someone else's opportunity to grow. When you stop rescuing, you start giving people the space to step up. And you reclaim your own energy, clarity, and peace.

Reflection

Who do I consistently "help" even when they don't ask for it?

_____

_____

_____

_____

_____

What would change if I let them figure it out on their own?

_____

_____

_____

_____

_____

When was the last time I felt resentful after helping someone? What does that tell me?

_____

_____

_____

_____

_____

Chapter 2

Boundaries Are Not Walls

How to say "no" without shutting people out.

Many people confuse boundaries with rejection. But boundaries aren't walls to keep people out—they're fences that protect what matters inside.

A boundary is simply a clear decision about what you will or won't allow in your life.

Examples of Healthy Boundaries

- "I'm happy to listen, but I won't be yelled at."
- "I'm unavailable after 6 p.m. so I can be present with my family."
- "I care about you, but I won't lie for you."

Tool: Boundary Script Template

"When you [behavior], I feel [emotion]. So, I will [boundary]."

Real-Life Story (Friendship)

Carlos's friend constantly vented about drama but never took advice. Carlos felt drained after every conversation. He finally said, "I care about you, but I can't keep having the same conversation over and over. Let's take a break from this topic." Their friendship didn't end—it got healthier.

Real-Life Story (Workplace)

Natalie, a team leader, kept getting messages from her boss late at night. She felt pressure to respond right away. After months of stress, she finally said, "I value quick communication, but I unplug after 6 p.m. to recharge. I'll respond first thing in the morning." Her boss adjusted—and Natalie slept better.

Real-Life Story (Family)

Rob's sister constantly asked for money. Every time he said no, she'd guilt him with, "You know I'm struggling." For years, Rob gave in—until one day he said, "I love you, but I'm no longer able to support you financially. I can help you look for resources, but I won't give cash." She got angry—but over time, she figured things out on her own.

Setting boundaries isn't easy. It's often met with pushback, especially from people who benefited from your lack of boundaries.

But that doesn't mean the boundary is wrong. It means it's working.

Tool: Resistance Response Guide

When someone resists your boundary, try:

- "I hear you. This is still my boundary."
- "I understand it's frustrating. And it's still what I need."
- "You don't have to agree. But I'm standing by this."

Key Takeaway
Boundaries create safety—for both people. They say, "This is where I end, and you begin." That clarity is the foundation for healthy, honest connection.

Reflection

Where in my life do I feel walked on or drained?

_____

_____

_____

_____

_____

What boundary would change that?

_____

_____

_____

_____

What fear is holding me back from setting it?

_____

_____

_____

_____

Chapter 3

Enabling vs. Empowering

How to help without harming.

There's a fine line between helping someone and holding them back. That line is the difference between enabling and empowering.

Enabling is doing for others what they can—and should—do for themselves. Empowering is supporting others as they do it for themselves.

Real-Life Story (Family)

Tina's adult son, Alex, struggled to keep a job. Every time he was fired, he moved back in and borrowed money. Tina thought she was being a loving mom by saying "yes." But after years of this pattern, she realized she wasn't helping— she was enabling. When she finally said "no" and held firm, Alex got a job, paid off debt, and moved out permanently. It was the wake-up call he needed.

Real-Life Story (Manager)

David managed a small team. Whenever one team member dropped the ball, David fixed it. He stayed late, corrected mistakes, and smoothed things over with clients. But performance never improved. After coaching with a mentor, David stopped stepping in. Instead, he held the team accountable. At first, there were more mistakes—but over time, everyone grew more capable and responsible.

Empowerment can be uncomfortable. You must tolerate short-term discomfort for long-term growth.

Tool: The Empowerment Filter

Before you help, ask yourself:

- Is this something they could do themselves?
- Am I stepping in to avoid my own discomfort?
- Will this action teach them something—or delay their growth?

If your answer shows you are enabling, step back and offer support without taking over.

Empowering Phrases

- "I believe you can handle this."
- "I'm here to support, not solve."
- "What's your next step?"

Key Takeaway
Empowerment is an act of trust. It says, "I believe in you enough to let you struggle, grow, and succeed on your own terms." It's not neglect—it's respect.

Reflection

Where in my life am I consistently rescuing someone?

_____

_____

_____

_____

_____

What would change if I stepped back and let them take the lead?

_____

_____

_____

_____

_____

What's the fear behind my need to fix?

_____

_____

_____

_____

_____

CHAPTER 4

Emotional Ownership

Why we are not responsible for other people's feelings.

One of the hardest truths to accept is this: you are not responsible for other people's emotions.

You can be kind, clear, and respectful—and they still might get upset. You can be generous—and they might still feel disappointed. You can say "no"—and they might feel hurt.

That's okay. Their emotions are theirs to own.

Real-Life Story (Family)

Jenna told her mom she wouldn't be coming home for the holidays this year. Her mom burst into tears and said, "I guess family doesn't matter to you anymore." Jenna almost caved— but instead she replied, "I love you. But I need to spend the holidays at my home this year." Her mom's reaction was painful, but Jenna learned that guilt wasn't a good reason to sacrifice her well-being.

Real-Life Story (Friendships)

Amir stopped replying immediately to every text. His friends noticed. "You've changed," one said accusingly. Amir explained he was prioritizing rest and focus. Not everyone understood—but over time, the ones who mattered respected his boundaries.

When you take ownership of someone else's emotions, you rob them of their autonomy—and burden yourself with their baggage.

Tool: The Emotional Fence

Visualize a fence between you and the other person. You can reach across to connect, but you don't climb over and try to fix their side.

What emotional ownership looks like:

- Letting others be disappointed without rushing to make it better
- Allowing anger to be expressed without absorbing it as your fault
- Holding space for sadness without needing to solve it

Key Takeaway

Taking ownership of your emotions—not theirs—is a skill that frees you. It allows you to show up with compassion instead of control. Presence instead of pressure. You are not their emotional caretaker. You are your own.

Reflection

When do I feel responsible for how others feel?

_____

_____

_____

_____

_____

What would change if I stopped trying to manage their emotions?

_____

_____

_____

_____

_____

How do I react when someone is upset with me?

_____

_____

_____

_____

_____

CHAPTER 5

The Guilt Reflex

Why we sometimes feel guilty.

Guilt is a powerful motivator—but sometimes it can be a false alarm.

We may feel guilty when we set boundaries, say "no," or prioritize our needs. And because it feels bad, we assume we did something wrong.

But feeling guilty doesn't always mean you did something wrong. It may just mean you did something different.

Real-Life Story (Parenting)

Claire, a single mom, decided to spend one weekend a month alone to recharge. Her teenage daughter said, "So you'd rather be alone than with me?" Claire felt a wave of guilt—but she calmly replied, "I need time alone so I can be a better mom the rest of the time." She stuck to her plan. Over time, her daughter understood—and Claire had more patience and energy.

Real-Life Story (Friendship)

Marcus declined an invitation to help a friend move for the third weekend in a row. "You're the only one I can count on," the friend texted. Marcus nearly gave in out of guilt—but realized he was being manipulated. He replied, "I've helped the past two weekends, and I'm not available this time. I trust you'll figure it out." The friendship cooled—but Marcus felt free.

Tool: The Guilt Test

Ask yourself:

- Did I violate my values?
- Was I dishonest, disrespectful, or harmful?
- Or did I just disappoint someone by choosing myself?

If you didn't violate your values, then guilt is just discomfort—not a moral failure.

Helpful Reframes

- "I can care about someone and still say no."
- "Disappointing someone isn't the same as wronging them."
- "Choosing myself isn't selfish—it's self-respect."

Key Takeaway
Learning to tolerate guilt is a key part of growing into emotional maturity. It means you're living with intention—not obligation. Let guilt be a signal—not a sentence.

Reflection

What situations tend to trigger guilt in me?

\
\
\
\
\

Is the guilt based on someone else's expectations or my own?

\
\
\
\
\

How do I typically respond when I feel guilty?

\
\
\
\
\

CHAPTER 6

When Helping Becomes Control

Why sometimes the best way to help is to get out of the way.

Sometimes helping isn't about kindness—it's about control.

It might not feel that way. You think you're just being helpful, supportive, or proactive. But if you look closely, some "helping" is actually about keeping things comfortable, predictable, or dependent on you.

Real-Life Story (Parenting)

Rachel always double-checked her son's backpack every morning, even in high school. "I just don't want him to forget anything," she said. But when her son left his science project at home one day, Rachel rushed it to school. Later, he shrugged and said, "Thanks. I knew you'd bring it." That's when it hit her—her "help" was training him not to take responsibility.

Real-Life Story (Workplace)

Ethan ran a tight ship as a department head. He checked every deliverable, corrected everyone's mistakes, and approved every decision. His team learned to rely on him for everything. Eventually, Ethan burned out. When he tried to delegate, his team froze—they hadn't learned to think for themselves.

Tool: The Motive Check

Ask yourself:

- Am I helping because I was asked—or because I can't handle how slow or messy it might be?
- Am I offering support—or trying to stay in control?
- Would I be okay if they failed a little but learned a lot?

Helping becomes control when you step in, not because someone needs you—but because *you* need to feel needed.

Helpful Reframes

- "It's okay if they struggle. That's how growth happens."
- "My discomfort doesn't mean I should interfere."
- "Support isn't control. I can care without micromanaging."

Real-Life Story (Friendship)

Nina often planned every outing for her friend group. She picked the restaurants, made the reservations, reminded everyone of the time. When she stopped organizing for a month, no one else stepped up. She realized she wasn't just helping—she was controlling the dynamic. When she let go, her friends began taking more initiative.

Control is subtle. It can wear the mask of being needed, helpful, or responsible. But it costs everyone involved:

- You become resentful.
- They become dependent.
- Growth is stunted on both sides.

Tool: The "Let-Go" List

Write down three things you routinely take over. Then ask:

- What would happen if I stopped doing this?
- What's the worst-case scenario—and could they recover from it?
- What lesson might they learn if I stepped back?

Letting go isn't abandoning—it's trusting. Trusting others to grow. Trusting yourself to stop fixing everything.

Key Takeaway
True help is rooted in respect.
It gives others space to learn, fail, and flourish.
And sometimes the best way to help is to get out of the way.

Reflection

Where do I over-function to feel in control?

_____

_____

_____

_____

_____

What am I afraid would happen if I stopped helping?

_____

_____

_____

_____

_____

Where can I start letting go today?

_____

_____

_____

_____

_____

CHAPTER 7

The Myth of Martyrdom

Why you don't have to earn your worth through burnout.

Somewhere along the way, many of us learned that being selfless means being exhausted. We think that love of others means always putting ourselves last.

But here's the truth: chronic self-sacrifice isn't noble—it's unsustainable. And often, it's not even truly selfless because it is driven by guilt, fear, or a need for approval.

Real-Life Story (Workplace)

Dana worked in a nonprofit organization and routinely stayed late to pick up the slack. She skipped lunch, covered shifts, and never used her vacation days. Everyone praised her dedication—until she landed in the hospital with stress-induced exhaustion. Her absence caused more chaos than her presence ever prevented. That's when Dana realized: if you're the glue holding everything together, you've become a single point of failure.

Real-Life Story (Family)

Tom always put his family's needs first. He took on extra jobs, managed the household, and made sure his kids never wanted for anything. But he never took care of himself. His wife finally said, "We don't need a hero. We need *you*—healthy, present, and not burned out." That conversation changed everything.

Martyrdom sends the message: "I don't matter." And people will believe you.

Signs of Martyr Mode
- Saying "yes" when you want to say "no."
- Being secretly resentful of those you help.
- Expecting others to notice or reciprocate your sacrifices.

Tool: The Self-Check Scale
On a scale of 1–10, ask yourself:

- How rested am I?
- How resentful am I?
- How often am I doing things I *want* to do?

If your resentment is high and rest is low, you're not being selfless—you're being self-forgetting.

Helpful Reframes
- "I can be generous without being depleted."
- "Taking care of myself is a gift to others."
- "Saying 'no' to them is saying 'yes' to my health, peace, and purpose."

Real-Life Story (Community/Church)
Angela volunteered for every church committee. She baked, organized, cleaned, taught, and led. People admired her. But she started to dread every meeting and fantasized about quitting. Her pastor said, "What would it look like to serve from joy instead of obligation?" Angela stepped back. She chose one committee she truly loved. Her energy and joy returned.

Serving others should energize, not deplete. When you operate from overflow, you can give freely. When you give from emptiness, you burn out—and sometimes, secretly hope someone notices and thanks you.

Tool: The "Enough" Filter

Before saying yes, ask:

- Is this mine to do?
- Do I want to do it—or do I feel like I *should*?
- Will this decision create peace or pressure in my life?

Key Takeaway
You are allowed to matter.
You don't have to earn your worth through burnout.
You can stop being a martyr and start being whole.

Reflection

What am I doing out of guilt instead of love?

_____

_____

_____

_____

_____

What would it look like to serve from joy, rather than obligation?

_____

_____

_____

_____

_____

How can I start honoring my limits?

_____

_____

_____

_____

_____

CHAPTER 8

Letting People Learn the Hard Way

How to let people face the consequences of their actions.

It is uncomfortable to watch someone you care about make mistakes. But sometimes, stepping in delays the lesson they need to learn.

One of the hardest forms of love is letting someone face the consequences of their actions.

Real-Life Story (Parenting)

Samantha's teenage son, Josh, routinely skipped studying. She used to nag, make flashcards, and sit beside him to help him focus. But his grades still slipped. One semester, she let go. He failed a major exam. Embarrassed and frustrated, he finally admitted, "I blew it." That failure motivated him more than all her reminders ever had.

Real-Life Story (Friendship)

Jared's best friend repeatedly ignored budgeting advice and kept overspending. Jared bailed him out twice, but the cycle continued. The third time, Jared said, "I love you, but I won't fix this for you again." His friend was angry—but later admitted that being cut off forced him to finally get help with his finances.

Pain is a powerful teacher. Trying to shield someone from it can keep them stuck.

Tool: The "Hard-Way" Compass

Ask yourself:

- Have I said what needed to be said?
- Have I modeled a better way?
- Am I trying to rescue someone from reality—or walk beside them through it?

When you've done your part, the rest is up to them.

Helpful Reframes

- "This isn't punishment. It's reality."
- "They are capable of learning from this."
- "I can care deeply without interfering."

Real-Life Story (Workplace)

Melissa, a team leader, used to step in whenever her junior teammate, Brian, missed deadlines. She'd rewrite his emails, fix his mistakes, and smooth things over with clients. One day, her supervisor said, "You're not managing him—you're babysitting him." Melissa let Brian face the consequences of a missed deadline. He was embarrassed—but started asking better questions and improved quickly. He grew because she let go.

Letting people learn the hard way isn't cruel. It's courageous.

Tool: "I Trust You" Statements

Instead of solving, say:

- "I trust you'll figure this out."
- "Let me know how it goes."

- "I'm here if you want to talk through it—but I'm not going to do it for you."

Key Takeaway

Sometimes love means letting people fall. Not to watch them suffer—but to give them the dignity of their own growth. That's not abandonment. It's belief in their ability to rise.

Reflection

Where am I stepping in too quickly?

_____

_____

_____

_____

_____

What am I afraid will happen if I don't intervene?

_____

_____

_____

_____

_____

What lessons might they learn if I step back?

_____

_____

_____

_____

_____

CONCLUSION

Freedom in Responsibility

Throughout this book, we've explored what happens when you stop taking on what isn't yours—and fully embrace what *is*.

We've looked at boundaries, enabling, emotional ownership, guilt, control, martyrdom, and the courage it takes to let people grow the hard way. Behind every lesson is the same truth: you are responsible for your own life, not anyone else's. And that's good news.

When you let go of what doesn't belong to you—other people's emotions, expectations, mistakes, and paths—you create space to:

- Show up more honestly.
- Love more freely.
- Rest more deeply.
- Grow more boldly.

Letting go doesn't mean you stop caring. It means you care in a cleaner, more sustainable way. It means you:

- Support, but don't rescue.
- Care, but don't control.
- Listen, but don't absorb.

This way of living is quieter, simpler, and infinitely freer.

- You are not here to fix everyone. You are not responsible for their happiness, healing, or growth.

- You are responsible for your words, your actions, your boundaries, your peace.

Own that fully. Let the rest go.

That's where real freedom begins.

Final Reflection Questions

What burdens have I been carrying that were never mine to begin with?

_____

_____

_____

_____

_____

What would it feel like to release them?

_____

_____

_____

_____

_____

What could I do with all the energy I've spent managing other people's lives?

_____

_____

_____

_____

_____

Other Books in This Series

Your Problem Isn't Your Problem. Solve the right problem. Solve the root cause rather than treat symptoms.

> *What if the problem you're trying to solve isn't the real problem? Learn to distinguish between symptoms and causes. Challenge assumptions that limit your thinking. Take action that solves the root cause of problems.*

My Problem Isn't Your Problem. Take responsibility for your problems. Don't blame, deflect, or expect others to fix your problems

> *Learn how to replace blame with responsibility, let go of excuses, and take real action at work, at home, and in your relationships. Shift from a victim mindset to one of leadership and agency.*

Your Problem Isn't My Problem. Set healthy boundaries. Stop rescuing others and allow them to solve their own problems.

> *Understand when to help others and when to step back. Learn about setting boundaries, detaching emotionally from others' outcomes, and supporting others without enabling bad behavior.*

About the Author

Larry Richman is a writer, speaker, and personal development coach known for his clear, practical approach to solving real-life challenges. With decades of experience helping individuals and organizations grow, he specializes in cutting through confusion to get to the heart of what really matters. His writing is refreshingly direct, relatable, and filled with tools you can use today to create lasting change.

www.ingramcontent.com/pod-product-compliance
Lightning Source LLC
Chambersburg PA
CBHW060950050426
42337CB00052B/3448